THE ART OF GETTING EVERYTHING

ADVANCE PRAISE

Suárez's book provides both the guidance and the how of balancing career, family and interest in work and life. She defines bringing these three areas together as creating our path. The author acknowledges that there is no single way of creating this path because we are different. Yet she provides critical tools to help us recognize what are the components that help to define what path to select.

Important among these tools are negotiation skills and active listening. In addition, the author includes multiple case examples of how these tools are applied. This practical approach makes this book one that is easy to apply and benefit from.

Suárez's coaching experience permeates the book with an approach that creates the sense that the reader is receiving individually tailored advice. A must read for anyone seeking ways of balancing work, family and interest to make life more fulfilling.

DR. ESTELA LOPEZ
Retired Provost
Connecticut State College & Universities Systems

Through examples and straightforward guidance, the author helps you to reframe your perspective and assess what truly matters - both personally and professionally. It's not necessarily about the good jobs, great education or personal relationships - it's the combination of them all that holds the magic. It's so easy to get caught up in the rat race, but this book reminds you that there are so many elements that go into having a successful LIFE. As a female 30-something, I needed this book, and the author's authenticity, to change direction and begin looking at my life in a new light.

SUZANNE SABLE
Communication Specialist
Social Change Sector

Elizabeth Suárez's new book, *The Art of Getting Everything*, is both relevant and pragmatic! The Results Strategist offers heart felt advice and genuine wisdom to Millennial professionals as they begin to develop their path, understand negotiations and manage net worth - Career, Family, and Interests. I recommend this book to Millennials who want to take note from the accomplished Author who paid her dues and is willing to share her vast knowledge and elaborate proven techniques.

LIZ ANTRY
Marketing and Communications Consultant

I really found this book to be fantastic! It made me think about the importance of truly managing my "net worth". As a successful business owner in the import/export international trade industry, I found the material to be so relevant on how to succeed not only professionally but also personally. I now have intimate knowledge on how to develop, grow and sustain a path that will translate into success. The real life-examples presented in the book provide a true understanding of the topic and makes the reader realize he/she is capable of reaching their own successful outcome.

GRISEL PADILLA, CHB, CCS
Founder & General Manager
G. Padilla & Co. International Trade Company

Although The *Art of Getting Everything* is focused on millennial professional women, I found this book applicable to women in just about any stage of life: from planning a career to planning retirement. Advice in this book will be valuable to me in the coming weeks (interviewing architects for my Caribbean home), months (financial advisors), and God willing, years (volunteering for and maybe leading projects that interest me). I highly recommend it to my millennial nieces, who are finding their paths.

JOAN LEWIS
Military Mom

Terrific topic! I wish I had this book when I started out in the real world, because they sure don't teach these real world ideas in school.

RONI LAMBRECHT
Author, *Parenting At Your Best*

THE ART OF GETTING EVERYTHING

HOW TO NEGOTIATE FOR WHAT YOU WANT **AND MORE**

ELIZABETH SUÁREZ

NEW YORK

NASHVILLE • MELBOURNE • VANCOUVER

THE ART OF GETTING EVERYTHING

HOW TO NEGOTIATE FOR WHAT YOU WANT **AND MORE**

Published in New York, New York, by Morgan James Publishing. Morgan James is a trademark of Morgan James, LLC. www.MorganJamesPublishing.com

The Morgan James Speakers Group can bring authors to your live event. For more information or to book an event visit The Morgan James Speakers Group at www.TheMorganJamesSpeakersGroup.com.

ISBN 9781683503798 paperback
ISBN 9781683503804 eBook
Library of Congress Control Number:
2016919729

Cover Design by:
Chris Treccani
www.3dogdesign.net

Interior Design by:
Chris Treccani
www.3dogdesign.net

In an effort to support local communities, raise awareness and funds, Morgan James Publishing donates a percentage of all book sales for the life of each book to Habitat for Humanity Peninsula and Greater Williamsburg.

Get involved today! Visit
www.MorganJamesBuilds.com

CONTENTS

I'M READY, BUT AM I TRULY PREPARED?

S ince I was a young girl, I had the dream and desire to be powerful. As the child of Cuban immigrants who struggled financially and emotionally to raise their family in Puerto Rico, I learned the importance of power very early in life. Although I had highly educated parents, they never seemed to have the necessary power or authority to easily succeed in life. It always appeared as if they were just treading water—never able to catch up or get ahead. Their experiences made me question the importance of education. Shouldn't education be the necessary variable for success? Isn't education essential to getting on the right path? I believe education is a must in today's world. However, I realized education without a complementary strategic path will only provide net worth that fails to go beyond financials.

Used in this context, net worth refers to the full package an individual must strive for and cultivate to reach success throughout life. Thus, net worth is not solely related to monetary values and financial freedom—although these are often important elements—rather, fulfilling your life goals is the focus. To holistically assess your net worth, you must take into account all of the pieces that affect your life including your career, family, and interests.

For over a decade, I have mentored a number of educated professional women. Regardless of their richly diverse backgrounds, skills, and beliefs they all have one thing in common: not knowing the importance of building a path to reach their desired net worth. Let's take Alexandra as an example. She is a twenty-six-year-old highly motivated professional, whose career interests are very similar to her personal interests. Like many other millennials, Alexandra not only wants to have a good paying job, she also wants to make a difference in her community. She is willing to work long hours if there is also time for her to be involved in a variety of social issues and interests. This includes leadership opportunities and continued education as well as nurturing children and families in need. Lastly, she also wants to have the time to focus on living healthy by eating nutritious meals and exercising. However, since attaining her college degree, she has been primarily focused on holding a job in order to pay for her student loans, rent, car payments, and general living expenses. She has not taken the time to outline her future path based on her interests, the wants for her family, and her career aspirations, all of which we are considering her net worth. For purposes of this book, I have used the work from researchers Neil Howe and William Strauss to describe millennials as the group "born between the year 1982 and 2000."

When I received a call from Alexandra about different non-profits in the community offering an array of leadership programs regarding legislation and politics, I asked a question that stumped her. "What will you get from these experiences to help you three years from now?" After asking her a few more questions, I realized I've had very similar conversations with other young women in recent years. Some of the answers I had received varied from, "I just need a job now because I have loans and bills to pay" to "three years from now is not on my radar; that is so far away."

Unfortunately, none of these answers are correct if we are considering one's net worth. To properly negotiate and manage your personal and professional wants and needs, you need to know your path. After discussing her net worth, Alexandra realized that creating a path was going to help her bring together her love of leadership and community with her career and financial expectations. She was aspiring to reach her net worth by uniting her professional expectations with family and personal interests.

I have built and updated my path throughout the years; however, I wish someone had shared this advice and wisdom with me when I was younger. My path was developed based on pure necessity and desperation. Even as a double Ivy League diploma recipient, I was stunned that the "field of dreams" was not readily available. I took too many long roads that led to a dead end. Luckily, these dead-ends didn't sway me from continuing on my journey. Instead, I learned from my choices and now I want to make sure you and others can too.

By highlighting personal and client examples, this book offers guidance and direction on developing your path and how to negotiate and manage your net worth once you have defined it.

CHAPTER 1
MAKING A DIFFERENCE

I am amazed at how few of us take the time to figure out our path in life. I must admit, however, that I did not figure out my own path until I had spent more than a decade working for several companies in corporate America. To be able to negotiate your net worth—which refers to an individual's full package (career, family, and interests)—you need to know what you want because without knowing the goal there is no place for negotiation. Although I had a great education, as time went by, I found myself just struggling to figure out what direction my career should be taking, and how it could complement my life. After all, I was just focusing on having a job with good compensation and benefits. I never thought about other things in my life such as my own interests and how they should interact with my professional track. Due to this, I was not able to talk to my bosses about my short- and long-term interests and how they could possibly connect with my career trajectory.

My first job out of college was magnificent. I worked for a Fortune 100 company as an engineer providing my expertise to multiple manufacturing plants across the country. I was given managerial and budgetary responsibilities. It was a fascinating experience, and it was that job which prompted me to apply to business school and expand my horizons beyond engineering. Unfortunately, I was still lost during business school and forged ahead without direction like several others in my class. My goal, as well as that of my classmates, was to secure a high paying position. I came from a generation where the value of money and independence was very high. Therefore, I placed a strong focus on my career and education in order to secure high-paying positions.

As such, I spent a few years working with investment bankers who felt entitled to six-digit salaries in 1990, a year when the United States was experiencing a recession.

After graduation, I also secured a six-digit salary and thought I had fulfilled my goals. In reality, I had no idea what I was doing to ensure I could have a great career as well as a fulfilling life. I remember my first day on the job as a graduate MBA professional. While it seemed like I had reached my goal, making over $100,000 and sitting in an office with a view, I did not *feel* anything. I wanted to make a difference and standing there I wondered if I was. I asked myself, "What is my amazing education going to do for me to make a difference not only in my professional life but also in my overall life?" How could I possibly be involved with interesting opportunities, such as community events, when I was working twelve-hour days? I sat in my chair wishing there was a guidebook for how to establish a realistic plan. Then I turned thirty, planned a wedding, days turned into months and months into years, not knowing why or what I was staying for. Inside the office, I was a professional woman not able to get what I wanted because I did not know how to negotiate for a full life where career, family, and interests were in unison. I began to worry about my future.

On January 1, 1995, I woke up and said to myself, "¡Basta, no más!" (Enough!). My husband and I spent the day figuring out what our future needed to be if we wanted to continue growing and evolving as a couple and family. After having very difficult discussions about what we really wanted, it was apparent that a path needed to be paved to ensure that we reached our goals. As a couple, we chose to work on our own individual paths. We ensured our paths complemented each other's and focused on our final goal as a couple: being happy and financially stable.

Our paths included personal and professional objectives, from expanding our family and taking care of our elders, to community involvement, developing stronger friendships, and leading a healthy lifestyle. It was on that New Year's Day that we decided there were many things that needed to change in our lives in order to reach our ultimate goals, both as individuals and as a couple. To get there, we both realized we needed to create a path. Although we had made important decisions and identified a long list of things to do, we understood this was not going to be accomplished in one day, a week, or even a month. This effort was going to be long-term and constantly updated. We realized that knowing what you want in your life is important because once you identify it, you can develop and negotiate your own path. This, in turn, provides you with your desired net worth.

When my husband and I figured out our own paths, we acknowledged the need to move to the western part of the country where it is easier to manage career and interests as a joint effort. We moved to the Denver Metro area, which is known for its outdoor lifestyle as well as friendly environment. My husband and I wanted to continue growing in our careers but also desired to have an active extracurricular life that included hobbies, such as hiking, biking, and skiing, as well as more time to spend with family and friends. We also enjoyed the performing arts scene where we could attend national touring performances and have access to a variety of galleries, museums, and dining venues. When I began working for a telecommunications firm as their business development executive, I was able to talk about my interests outside the workplace with my boss for the first time. At first, I thought he might not welcome this type of conversation, but it was the opposite. These conversations turned into discussing what I was passionate about in life and identifying networks and people I needed to reach out to to get connected. Although my husband had shifted his work to be a fulltime telecommuter for his East Coast employer, he also had the experience of discussing these important issues with new friends and colleagues he met in our new home.

My experience developing and implementing my own path has made it possible for me to coach several professionals during the past decade. I have had several clients who have stayed in their jobs and negotiated more balance into their lives, and I have had clients leave their work seeking a more balanced life. One client, a scientist for a large global pharmaceutical corporation, had never taken the time to even consider having a defined path. Instead, her focus was how long it would take her to get promoted to the next level. She did this so efficiently that she was getting promoted almost every eighteen months. Each promotion brought larger compensation, an amazing title, more responsibilities, and less time for fun. When I first sat down with her to discuss her interests, she broke down. She shared with me how she'd never taken the time to consider what she really wanted in life as a whole. Therefore, when I asked her to share what path she would take to reach her desired net worth, she became embarrassed and angry that she wasn't able to provide an answer. As an executive in a large global company, she thought she should have the answers to all the questions.

Similar to my client, my husband and I took the time to discuss and contemplate what our lives needed to look like for us to feel fulfilled and happy. During this time, we would often think about what stories we wanted to share with family once we were elderly. We certainly did not want to just speak about jobs. We wanted to be able to talk about the travel and adventures we lived, and how we met so many fascinating people throughout our lives. For this to happen, we first needed to create our path so we could then negotiate and advocate for it.

CHAPTER 2
CREATE YOUR OWN PATH

Developing and implementing a path to navigate through life and determine your overall net worth is important. For starters, your net worth is not just dealing with financial status. It includes an array of elements that include: income, personal assets, knowledge, skills, family, community, health, and personal satisfaction/ interests. I suppose you would agree that all of these points are important to be considered throughout our lives. During different phases of our lives, some will overshadow others. However, it is essential that while we grow as individuals we ensure all are being considered and addressed.

If managing our net worth is so important, you would think most of us would take more time to cultivate the individual elements. On the contrary, I would argue that very few of us have taken the time to create a path to effectively manage our own ideal and balanced life. We meet with advisors, mentors, and colleagues, and we are fully aware that it is our responsibility to manage our future. If we know this, why aren't we implementing this approach in our own lives? We must not be taking the time to figure out our goals in order to strive for something more. Let me state here that striving for more is an essential practice of any successful person. Nevertheless, it seems that people simply dream and forget to really create and execute a plan to make their dreams a reality. Being complacent does not produce opportunity and growth. It just meets the status quo. Sometimes status quo is all you want, but I bet any hard-working professional like you is always wanting and seeking for more. If that is the case, it is time to work on building your own path!

How do you build a successful path? Is there a realistic formula or method you can use? My answer to these questions is yes and no. Yes, because there are steps that any person can follow. No, because the steps are not the same for every individual. It requires work to customize and mold your own approach. Like building a neighborhood of houses, there is always a blueprint that a construction crew follows to build the homes. However, once the homes are sold to their respective owners, the houses take on a life of their own. They might have a different look due to a variety of paints, materials, and decorations. The homes were constructed based on a list of guidelines and instructions, but they ended up being different due to the people involved in the process. Everyone is different and these differences are what make the various paths a work of art. Borrowing somebody else's exact method might not get you to your end goal. Hence, it is imperative that we all take the time to assess our current and future needs and desires before we begin constructing our own paths.

To begin creating your path, you must first consider three pieces of your life on an equal basis: your professional career and ambitions, your family, and your interests or hobbies that fulfill your life. Ideally, these three pieces need to congeal and intertwine equally with each other as you map out your own path. On occasion, you might place stronger weight on one over the other, but as a whole you focus on making sure all pieces are considered and addressed throughout your life.

If a person focuses on just one of these pieces, they will lose sight of their larger goals. This is exactly what happened to Alexandra. After celebrating her twenty-sixth birthday, she felt the need to place a strong focus on her career. She began questioning why she was working at her current employer. She felt as if everyday was a drag and not fulfilling. She sensed she was not getting what she needed to succeed and become a better individual. However, if asked to define exactly what she needed, she couldn't offer a concrete response. Instead, she would find the negative in everything and everyone that surrounded her. When her supervisor decided to retire—a mentor that had taken an interest in her career—Alexandra felt it was another sign for her to leave the organization. It was at that time that she reached out to me for advice.

Our first meeting was full of energy, laughter, and stories. It had been several years since I had seen her, and there was a lot of catching up to do. The last time I had seen Alexandra, she was in the middle of college and moving to another state. The four or more years apart seemed to melt away as we shared our stories and experiences. It was during that encounter when I noticed Alexandra was very driven and wanted to succeed both personally and professionally. Additionally, I noticed she was acting like a lost child in a candy store; too many options available to her with no idea how to prioritize and choose. Our conversation jumped around from wondering about community leadership programs to figuring out the best negotiation techniques to asking for a raise or getting a new job. I encouraged Alexandra to segment her thinking into buckets where she could identify interests and prioritize between immediate and long-term needs and desires.

During our follow up conversations, the topic of discussion became more focused. Alexandra had decided to actively seek new employment that provided her with the opportunity to make a difference in her community while embracing different leadership prospects and learning about new fields, education, and non-profits. We spent the most time on subjects concerning her goals that related to the three pieces included in the method for building her path. She had recently gotten engaged, and now there was another person to consider in her goal setting and decision-making. This was yet another reason why she needed to focus on figuring out what needed to be included in her path.

With the experience of mentoring Alexandra as well as coaching multiple professional individuals, I have witnessed firsthand how long-term vision normally suffers during a decision point in somebody's life. For instance, imagine you are at a crossroads where you need to make a decision to stay with your current employer or pursue a different opportunity that has come your way. In Alexandra's case, the opportunity was to join a nine-month leadership program, which required several days of time-off from work. Similar to Alexandra's, the opportunity sounds challenging but fun, and it aligns with your interests. After all, you have been in the same position for over a year and you are becoming bored of the job and your colleagues. In addition, you have been wanting a raise or title change and nothing has materialized. It seems this new opportunity can provide you with access to a new network of leaders and potential future employers.

What should you do? Go for it, right? Not so fast! Before even inquiring about the opportunity, I suggest you assess where you are in your path. Have you taken the time to determine what type of path to build? Have you determined what is important now and how it can change in the future? If you are having difficulties answering these questions, I recommend you download an infographic from my website, elizabethsuarez.com, that addresses the three pieces to include in your path. This document will assist you in thinking about what really matters to you and the people you love. When I used the infographic with Alexandra, I provided her with a challenging task. She took a few days to really think about the answers and questions we discussed. To assist her with the task, I recommended she carry a journal with her at all times. That way, when an answer, thought, or idea came to mind, she would be able to write it down and remember it later when she had more time to focus. Most of Alexandra's ideas came when she was exercising on the treadmill. I am still trying to figure out the visuals on this one. Good news: she never fell while recording her thoughts. That was a relief!

Many times when we are seeking advice it is related to one of the three elements of path creation: career. We go through our life mostly involved with work and might take for granted the two other pieces: family and interests. Although most of us proclaim that family and interests are our top priorities, in reality, few of us can show how we spend the necessary quality time to nourish them. I was truly impressed with how Alexandra tried to work on all three pieces. She worked long hours, spent time with her fiancé and still found time to lead a healthy lifestyle. She was committed to these elements no matter the hours they required. I am not suggesting that you begin exercising at midnight; instead, focus on being flexible with your time when determining how to accomplish all of your items that contribute to path development. By being so passionate about fulfilling her interests, Alexandra was able to perform at higher standards and be viewed as an essential leader. She came across as an accomplished individual, one who knew how to balance it all. People who surrounded her felt the positive energy she emitted.

There are many times when our career must be a priority to allow us to reach our goals as well as to simply pay our bills. This does not mean that you should make a decision about a job without figuring out how it complements and/ or affects the other two pieces of your net worth. I remember being recently married, living in the New York City metro area with an amazing job, a beautiful home, and a busy calendar of activities. Anybody that met me surely would have classified me as having it all. I had the husband, the career, the immediate family (two step-daughters), a beautiful home in the suburbs, and two new cars. However, deep inside, I was miserable. What was going on? I would cry on my way to and from work. On weekends, I would spend the days just sleeping or watching senseless TV shows to pass the time, not engaging or thinking about my life. I dreaded Monday mornings since I knew it was the beginning of another week without direction. I had a work plan and was an excellent performer with outstanding reviews. Despite these glowing achievements, I had no idea what my job's purpose was and where it would ultimately take me, what I would gain from it, and why I was working so hard. I could not visualize the final goal.

The morning of January 1, 1995, was when I knew I had to stop this madness. I could not continue to just exist. I had a great husband and an opportunity for a wonderful life, but I did not know how to navigate everything. I referenced before having the difficult conversations that morning that made my husband and me move across the country to a city neither one of us had ever lived in before but hoped was the right place for us to grow as a family. During those talks, we openly discussed our professions, families, and interests. We were desperate and knew we needed some kind of intervention. We were both in an environment where we didn't feel fulfilled and knew something needed to change. Obviously, we looked at career first since we needed the income to make the move. However, for the first time, we also discussed family and interests.

Our discussion focused on how we wanted to define ourselves as individuals over the next twenty years. The definition that we needed to provide included the three pieces of our individual paths. It sounds simpler than it actually was. Being analysis-driven people, we both focused on writing down all of what we wanted to undertake in the timeframe identified. We encouraged each other to highlight a similar amount of wishful undertakings for each piece in our path. Once we completed the task, we worked on determining how each of the items correlated with each of our other pieces. For instance, one of my goals for my family piece was to be able to have my own child. How did such a goal correlate with my interests? What about my profession? From the interest piece, my goal was to be fully involved in raising my child. From the professional piece, I wanted to continue moving up the corporate ladder. You may be wondering, how was I going to be able to do that? Aren't women in the higher ranks of corporate America fully dependent on nannies and spend several nights per week away from the home on business travel? Unfortunately, that was the reality I was facing. I did not want to just give up and sacrifice not having a child. For me, that was not an option. I forged ahead, had the child, hired the nanny, and went back to work. The only thing that saved me with this approach was the fact that we had already moved out of the NYC metro area. We had a better quality of life with a shorter commute time, and we were living closer to extended family. However, this phase quickly ended as I was suddenly facing another crossroads in my profession. My employer was bought out, and the new owners wanted me to move back to the East Coast. There were no other options offered, you said "yes" or you took the severance. Without much analysis, I took the severance and hoped for the best.

I remember going home and sharing the news with my husband. He was a trooper. He listened to my reasoning and tried to show his support. However, I knew he was not too pleased with the final outcome. After all, my oldest stepdaughter was heading to a private university and the second one was a junior in high school also considering her options for college. In two short years, we were going to have two young ladies in college with another one in day care. Imagine the amount of cash that would be needed from our household, and my influx of salary was suddenly cut off. This was not a good combination.

If my husband and I had not gone through the path building exercises back in January of 1995, I believe my first reaction and goal would have been to find another job that offered a similar salary to the one I had just walked away from. At first, I was overwhelmed with stress; I was not ready to have these conversations right after losing my job. Instead, I occupied my time with tasks that did not require much thinking. After some time, I realized I needed to have these conversations with my husband. We sat down and revisited our paths and evaluated how we were performing against our plan and spent time determining what needed to change. For starters, we reevaluated our main goals and assumptions. For us, it was imperative that we could continue saving and growing our financial nest egg while still being able to offer all three daughters the education and experience they needed. Since we did not want to modify this main goal, we needed to move toward discussing what else needed to change.

To create your path, you need to take into consideration the three pieces: career, family, and interests. Once you have mapped out these areas based on your wants in the short- and long-term, you will be able to negotiate on behalf of yourself and your pieces.

CHAPTER 3

GET YOURSELF IN ORDER

There I was, an experienced, young corporate professional collecting a severance having no clue what to do next. I had family and financial responsibilities that made me very aware I needed to continue working. Not only was I a mother of a toddler, but I also was the stepmother of two teenagers heading into college soon. Additionally, I was faced with an elderly mother who needed my help more and more each day. As a family-oriented individual, I took pride in being fully involved in the upbringing of my daughter, while being very hands-on in my mother's and stepdaughters' lives. My days consisted of multiple to-do lists, from doctor appointments and networking gatherings to high school sports games and homework. My husband was as invested as I was in the well-being of our family. We sought help from friends and family members, but at the end of the day we were the ones managing it all. This approach had worked beautifully since we got married. However, there was one major difference we were now facing: I was not contributing an income, and our financial responsibilities were about to double due to college tuition.

For the first six months after receiving my severance package, I solely focused on taking care of the family, sending out resumes and networking with everyone I could imagine. Several opportunities came across my desk, but in reality I was not ready to return to the workforce. I was not ready because I did not have myself in order. I knew I had to reassess my path. I had to ask myself where I was and if what I had outlined previously was still what I wanted to do.

When you jump headfirst into an opportunity without knowing if it falls in line with what you want for your family, interests, and career, you risk letting go of an area of your life that may be very important to you. This happened to me during a job after graduate business school. At the age of twenty-seven , I chose the job that offered me the highest salary and bonus. For me, it would be fabulous to have so much money that I could travel and live in a nice apartment. Little did I know there would be limited time for personal travel. I did not make the effort to truly analyze how this job would affect not only my career path but also allow me to manage my family and interests. Since I did not have an established path, I was also not having the necessary conversations about balance. Consequently, by taking this offer I became overworked and disgusted with my daily existence. My salary was fantastic, but I had no time to spend it. I could not even take the time to go shopping on a Saturday afternoon with a friend. Additionally, I was not able to take trips to visit my mother. At the time, she lived in another state and going to visit her required at least a few days. I ended up leaving that job after spending close to a half-year looking for another one. In my new job, I was able to balance all of the pieces as effectively as possible. In this position, I was able to join an exercise program as well as become part of a non-profit board. I even ended up planning a few vacations and trips to visit my mother.

Before you accept that wonderful job offer, take the time to analyze it and compare how it complements your path. If we take the first thing that comes to us, it is possible that it's right for the short-term, but not good for the long-term. My client, Katharina, did exactly that as she was evaluating an opportunity with a small organization in her hometown. She had spent the last decade working in high-power jobs across the nation and even internationally. She was a recognized legal professional; however, she had reached a point in her life where she was part of the sandwich generation. This meant she was responsible for the well-being of not only her two young children but also her elderly parents. In order to reach a realistic balance, she had taken the time to develop her path that identified the following key items for each piece.

Career:

- Six-digit salary with benefits and four to five weeks of vacation annually.
- A position with Profit & Liability (P&L) responsibility and a team of professionals to manage.
- A collaborative work environment where individuals are involved in decision-making.
- A company that is at the cutting edge of a particular field.

Family:

- Be an active family figure for her young daughters. Be able to see them play soccer, attend school field trips, and host sleepovers and birthday parties.
- Be able to put her daughters to bed at least twice during the week and during the weekend.
- Be there for her parents as they age.
- Have a caring relationship with her husband and have enough time for date nights at least twice a month.

Interests:

- Be able to participate in the Boston Marathon in the near future.
- Be able to go to the gym at least twice a week to train for the marathon.
- Be able to reconnect with her friends and spend some time learning a new hobby.
- Participate in a book club, wine collection group, or any other type of gathering where she could establish and grow friendships.

When Katharina was offered the job back in her hometown at the salary scale she was seeking, her gut instinct was to just accept the job. But after remembering her path, she knew better and placed a call to me. During the call, we discussed her path and identified the items she needed to discuss with her soon-to-be boss about fulfilling her goals. The key issue that came to light was her need to visit the gym twice a week. She definitely did not want to go very early in the morning, which would not allow her to take her daughters to school. She also did not favor exercising at midnight. After some discussion with her future boss, they were able to agree that no work meetings would be set for her after 4:30 p.m. This allowed her to leave at a reasonable time twice a week to hit the gym. Those evenings she found herself bringing work home. This behavior became a necessity to balance her career, family, and interests in order to fulfill her long-term goals.

Since Katharina referred back to her path when she received the offer, she was able to make the right decision to live the life she was seeking and working toward. I encourage you to take the time to analyze every opportunity. If you are offered a great job, it does not mean you have to accept it immediately. Instead, take the time needed to discuss with your partner, mentor, coach, and friend so you can effectively assess its advantages and disadvantages and make the right decision.

CHAPTER 4

LIFE IS ALL ABOUT NEGOTIATING

We have just learned the importance of having a path. For the next step, we must understand how to negotiate. This key skill will keep you on track with your developed path. How many of you have been in the situation where you are hoping to leave work early to participate in an extracurricular activity, but you are stopped by external factors at work? Perhaps your office is known for rewarding high-stress and long hours. Therefore, how do you ensure you can still balance your interests while performing your best? Typically, people will say, "It is not worth it. If it does not change, I will just leave the company." Instead, consider having a conversation with your boss about why this extracurricular activity will benefit the organization since it is a way for you to regain your energy and perform at your highest level. This does not mean you will not complete the tasks assigned. You will still do that while enjoying your extracurricular activity. You might complete the task at a later time in the evening or during another day. All of this is negotiable and worth talking about.

Women have never been viewed as good negotiators. In recent years, authors like Sheryl Sandberg (*Lean In*) as well as Linda Babcock & Sara Laschever (*Women Don't Ask: Negotiation and the Gender Divide*) provide a great look at what women must do to succeed in their careers and overall life. These readings mainly refer to scripted negotiations such as purchasing a home or applying for a job. However, most of us do not go through life always buying a home or negotiating a promotion. We do embark in several other conversations and activities, like leaving work early or working from home on Fridays. These are unscripted negotiations and still require similar skills. No matter the circumstance, women must feel comfortable negotiating with others, especially when it comes to the pieces on their path.

From the last three chapters, you know how important it is to define your path in order to begin to negotiate in the workplace. Now I am going to share with you the three key tips that can help you navigate any situation, no matter the topic: prepare, practice, and perspective.

Prepare

Before we engage in any conversation that requires negotiation, it is imperative that we prepare. While preparation takes place way before any interaction, it is easier to do when getting ready for a scripted negotiation. Regardless of the type of interaction, however, one must analyze the overall situation before any negotiation occurs. This includes understanding one's needs and desired outcomes and those of the opposing party. Luckily, preparing for scripted negotiations will help us during unscripted negotiations, which are rarely planned for and often catch us by surprise.

Examples of unscripted conversations can be found in the interest and family pieces. For instance, your partner wins a trip to Italy for a wine-tasting excursion in Tuscany. Both of you are avid wine connoisseurs. This trip was not planned, and it truly fulfills one of your bucket list items. Obviously, you want to join your partner in this once-in-a-lifetime experience. What should you do? You have a few vacation days left for the year, and you could borrow a couple days from the next year. It is time to prepare as if this was a scripted negotiation similar to purchasing a car or home. When getting ready to purchase a large item, you normally prepare by determining the needs and wants of all involved. If your significant other is feeling the need for a sports car, you might work on identifying the numerous advantages of owning one. These could include: Sunday afternoon drives, spending time together, overall happiness, and the cool factor. Use the same approach when you need to talk with your boss about the unexpected vacation. Why does it mean so much to you? How will you manage the work in your absence? And how will this benefit your productivity and, in turn, your department's output in the long run? By now, you have figured out the formula: you identify and nourish the benefits for the other party. It is not about focusing on your side and then playing the victim if you do not get your way.

Another instance when an unscripted negotiation opportunity could emerge is when you have agreed to play a supportive negotiator role in a situation but last minute changes forces you to take the lead. Recently, my husband

and I went through the process of purchasing a "manly" truck for him. As an avid outdoorsman, my husband needed a top-of-the-line vehicle that could go off-road and do well in urban settings. Our preparation for this scripted negotiation consisted of determining the best features needed as well as price points and the overall look. Like any other vehicle purchase, we first looked at the market value and then compared and contrasted dealerships prior to even visiting one. This preparation was extensive and detail-driven.

Once we arrived at the dealership, we opted to browse around the parking lot since there were so many trucks on display. We had our young daughter with us for input. There was a lot of discussion about color and overall comfort for the family when sitting in the truck. As expected, we were approached by a salesperson that offered his assistance. My husband kindly stated that we were just looking and would go into the showroom once we were ready.

As we entered the showroom, we were immediately approached by the salesperson we encountered outside. This individual began the conversation with, "Aren't these trucks all beauties? I can help you drive away with one today." My husband immediately answered with, "Great! I have a few questions about the different trucks." The salesperson proceeded to look directly at my husband when he stated,

"Great, come to my office so we can talk further and answer all of your questions." As we walked into his office, I knew it would be almost impossible to get the salesperson to include me in the conversation. He took a good five minutes explaining why they were the best dealership and the attributes of the truck model we were interested in. All of this information was directed to my husband. The salesperson concluded his sales pitch with, "Hope this information helped you make a decision. Are you ready to talk numbers?" My husband responded with, "Actually, you will need to speak with my wife since she is the one that deals with our finances and large purchases in our household." With that statement, my husband got up and walked out with our daughter. You should have seen the salesperson's face. He tried very hard to earn my trust as we began negotiating. I had just been given the edge and was able to demand the dealership's manager as my salesperson. Although my husband and I expected for the salesperson to place a stronger focus on him, I never expected to become the lead negotiator. All of a sudden, my supportive role became obsolete as I took the reigns to make the deal. Needless to say, we walked out with a new truck!

If I would have not prepared to fully understand what was at stake, I would have struggled knowing how to request a different salesperson and determine if this was the best deal in town. Throughout the negotiation process, I kept referring to the research and discussion my husband and I had about the truck. No matter what the salesperson would tell me, I maintained my focus on the desired price, and I was able to counter and keep the conversation on track, which allowed us to drive away with the truck paying a price very close to market value.

This type of preparation can be accomplished for more day-to-day unscripted negotiations such as where to go for lunch with a colleague, who will run the errand, or who will make the coffee in the morning. To get the most out of these daily negotiations you need to know whom you are regularly interacting with. Obviously your interactions with your spouse, close family member, or best friend are much more frequent and in-depth than those with your neighbor or a work colleague. Therefore, it might be much easier to understand the needs and wants of your closer allies when you participate in a discussion that requires some sort of decision. Nevertheless, even with the individuals that you might not mingle with as frequently, you need to prepare how to address them or even answer their request. Before responding allow yourself a moment to really listen to what they shared with you. This means you are able to recite the message they shared. If you are not ready for that, it is time to ask them for clarification by simply stating, "What I heard you saying is… Did I miss anything?" Many times, when someone asks this type of question it provides the other party an opportunity to hear their own message and determine if this is what they were trying to convey. Additionally, this offers a moment where all individuals are able to engage in further explanation, affording a better opportunity to hopefully reach a resolution. It also gives you some more information to better understand the other party's perspective. This way you are able to correlate it with your own and determine how to proceed in the discussion, even if it is about who makes the coffee on a rainy Saturday morning. Maybe it will be you, but you are able to gain something else in return like maybe dinner out that evening.

For every unscripted negotiation opportunity you might encounter without warning, I encourage you to identify a go-to sentence you can use to continue the conversation. Feel free to use the one I provided. It does work!

Practice

You are now ready to negotiate scripted as well as non-scripted conversations. But what if you tried it for the first time and it did not seem to work? The outcome turned out to be more one-sided. What went wrong? For starters, you might have come across as lacking confidence in your position and even hesitant. Why is that? Did you really prepare?

I recently had this exact conversation with one of my clients. There was a project being assigned that everyone had been trying to avoid. The project encompassed a lot of travel (over 60 percent). My client had worked very hard preparing to have this conversation about the project in the upcoming staff meeting. She understood the issues, needs, and wants of each of her co-workers. She even developed a grid that illustrated all of this information including different options on how to effectively manage the project. The options considered the well-being of all employees involved and even offered some ways on how to manage for the short- and long-terms. However, when my client shared her thoughts and ideas she realized her co-workers were not engaging or demonstrating any interest in cooperating with her proposal. She described it as if she was experiencing an "out-of-body experience," while words were coming out of her mouth, her mind was wondering why she was even talking. She wanted to stop speaking, but she could not stop.

You can work hard at creating and updating your path and preparing to begin any negotiation. If you do not practice the new ideas and approaches you are about to share, you won't come across as credible. This is what happened with my client. She had done her homework and worked hard at figuring out possible win-win solutions for all parties involved. However, she made one big mistake. She never practiced how she was going to deliver these new ideas. She did not take the time to rehearse how to open, position, and close the discussion with her colleagues. She had mapped out all of the alternatives and even figured out different ways to approach negative responses. But she never identified what exact words she was going to use and never practiced saying these words out loud. This is the reason why consultants, when providing training and coaching services, always include the dreaded role-plays. It allows parties the opportunity to act out a situation.

My client never took the time to have her ears listen to her own words. This simple act would have provided my client the capability of feeling comfortable delivering the message to her co-workers. Instead she came across as awkward. The next time you must deliver an important statement or partake in a negotiation take the time to practice your words and message. Ask a friend or colleague to role-play the situation. This extra time will produce a stronger outcome.

Perspective

According to merriam-webster.com, perspective is defined as "the interrelation in which a subject or its parts are mentally viewed." For example, if you think sugar destroys or ruins your health then, from your perspective, an ice cream parlor is not conducive to a healthy lifestyle. You can prepare and practice, but if you do not take the time to figure out the other party's perspective, it will be very difficult to reach an agreement.

During a recent contentious workplace mediation session, I was mediating two parties that could not be any further apart in their ideas and resolutions. We had reached a terrible impasse where one of the parties threatened to leave the mediation. I tried every trick available during our caucus sessions. However, the party was tired and felt disillusioned about the process. He stated, "I have done everything in my power to work toward a solution, but I feel the other party is not putting in as much effort as I am. So enough. I'm done." As he walked out, I followed him to further discuss his feelings. My intent was to determine some way to get him back to the mediation table. As we walked out the building together, it became evident that he felt as if he was compromising more than the other party. As the mediator, I did not agree with this statement. I actually thought both parties were equally vested in the mediation.

After convincing him to come back to the mediation, I placed both parties face to face at the table. Each party was convinced that they were right and the other one was wrong. No matter how much reasoning I tried to do with each party, I was not able to convince either one to take the time to understand the other's viewpoint. I gave each party a paper with a picture of a rectangle. I stated how each paper was the same. One paper had a yellow rectangle and the other had a black one. I asked each party to describe what they saw on their paper. Each went ahead and stated they had a rectangle on the paper. The first party mentioned that her rectangle was yellow. The other party thought she was nuts, since he had a black rectangle. They both looked at each other as if the other was crazy. They could not understand why the other party was saying something so wrong and different. I immediately requested them to exchange their paper and then asked them to describe what they saw on the new paper. They both realized it was the same object but in a different color.

This exercise illustrated to both parties that sometimes a problem or disagreement must be looked at from the other person's perspective. This will help any party better understand the other person's viewpoint. When involved in a negotiation, you need to understand how every person reaches a different conclusion based on that person's values and beliefs. You both could be seeing and reading the same information, but your interpretation is very different from each other's. Our brains are always establishing opinions about every experience or situation. Like author Anaïs Nin stated, "We don't see things as they are, we see things as we are" (1961, 124). Therefore, when you feel as if you are not getting anywhere in a negotiation, take some time to better understand the other person's perspective about the topic. This might require asking yourself in what other ways you can view the situation at hand.

When you are negotiating, no matter if it is scripted or unscripted, you must demonstrate that the other party's perspective is more important than your own. Stuart Diamond, the author of *Getting More*, states, "Anything you do in a negotiation should explicitly bring you closer to your goals for that particular negotiation" (2012, 6). In order to meet your goals, it is imperative that you fully understand and can meet the other party's perspective, even if you feel that they are wrong and you are right. Negotiation is not about figuring out who is right or wrong. It is about getting the parties involved to agree to embrace the other party's perspective.

After reading this chapter, you are aware of the three key points to any negotiation: prepare, practice, and perspective. First, you need to become prepared to know the needs and wants of the other person. After doing your homework, it is time to practice your approach. This means acting out what could happen before, during, and after the negotiation. This way you can listen to yourself and become comfortable saying and hearing the words you want to share with the other party. The third key is perspective. No matter how much you prepare and practice, if you are not able to understand that everybody will derive a different perspective from a similar activity or event, you won't be able to advance in your discussion. Before you begin communicating your thoughts and ideas, you must take the time to think how the other party will view them.

CHAPTER 5

MAKE ANY OFFER
WORK FOR YOU

I remember receiving Alexandra's call. She had been offered the job she wanted based on all the work we had done together when creating her path. She knew what her net worth should be, and she went after it. After a lot of hard work and multiple job interviews, at last she received an offer that would let her be part of the non-profit sector. She surely wanted to make a difference in her community. Plus, the job offer included higher compensation than what she was expecting. That was a major bonus! She was so excited on the call. After listening to her energized description of the offer, I asked her if she had accepted it. I was pleased to hear she had asked for some time to make a decision. She did reinforce to me that she would take the offer. It was too good to say no. Was it really that good of an offer? Did the offer complement Alexandra's path? In this chapter, we are going to examine how you can turn a great monetary opportunity into one that can truly fulfill your path and all of its pieces.

Career

Normally, job offers are very focused on the career piece. It is all about salary, benefits, and vacation time. Employers may use a compensation grid that identifies a pay scale. The grid may take into account the candidate's background, skills, education, and experience to identify a specific compensation amount. With some of the larger employers, the pay scale not only includes the salary but also the potential for an annual bonus and any other compensation, such as stock options and equity. The latter options are rarely available in the non-profit arena and, in recent years, they are not as readily available in for-profit sectors. However, I always encourage candidates to inquire about stock options and equity deals when negotiating in the for-profit arena, such as corporate

America and privately held businesses. Even though these alternatives might never be mentioned during a job offer, it is something that needs to be inquired about. The worst they could say is this type of compensation is not offered for your level. Follow-up such statement with, "At what level is it offered?" Don't be shy about asking this question; it is important information to know as you work hard and are rewarded with a higher position.

I remember when I received my first job offer from a medium-sized privately owned company. I had only worked in corporate America and was accustomed to receiving stock options, as well as having a professional development budget included in my offers. However, I knew that these items might not be part of an offer in a private sector firm. My offer came from a family-owned telecommunications company where salary scales and overall compensations were not discussed or known by the employees. The firm was recognized for its very collaborative environment where employees were fulfilled and happy with their work. When I received the job offer, I saw a line item making reference to an equity ownership. I was thrilled to see it. The rest of the offer was very competitive, and it even included an extra week of vacation since the owner felt his employees needed to have work-life balance. I quickly accepted the offer without question. Big mistake!

Although the offer was very lucrative and attractive, later I learned that I had left some money on the table. This is a very typical move for women when being offered a job. According to Linda Babcock, author of *Women Don't Ask*, women cap their salary growth by age thirty-seven and men by age forty-five. This translates to an average women's cap of $62,000 while men's cap is around $95,000. This means women need to work, on average, an extra eight years to reach men's wealth. Why such a large salary gap? Babcock writes that based on a research study of Carnegie Mellon University graduates with a master's degree when women graduates were offered a salary, only 7 percent negotiated the offer. Meanwhile over 57 percent of men negotiated the salary (Babcock and Laschever 2003, loc. 126). This is precisely what happened to me. I was so mesmerized by the offer that I did not take the time to negotiate. After all, it included a great salary and benefits, plus it took into account my path's family piece. A year into the job, I learned that my male colleague, who began working a month before me, was offered a salary 15 percent higher than mine and even 10 percent more for his professional development budget. Why was that? I had the same amount of experience, plus my educational background was stronger (I had a master's degree and a few more years of experience). The primary discrepancy: when my male colleague received the offer, he asked for more. He illustrated to the hiring manager the value of his background and overall skills while explaining how the organization could benefit. I, on the other hand, was just so pleased with the offer that my focus was placed on thanking them and figuring out when I could start working. Although I had my path developed, I really had not deployed my three negotiation tips: prepare, practice, and perspective. I thought I had prepared myself, but in reality I had no idea how compensation structure worked in privately held companies. Additionally, I had not spent the time practicing receiving and discussing an offer that would provide a positive surprise. And finally, I had no clue there could be a very different perspective when it came to comparing professional and educational backgrounds of individuals hired to do similar work. I felt my strong educational background with my vast corporate America experience would trump a professional with less years of experience and with limited corporate experience. I was certainly wrong and, in turn, could come across cocky and demanding.

Even today, with so much focus placed on women and negotiation, a gap still exists. Some women are negotiating and getting better at it, but we have a long road ahead of us. Take, for instance, this example from a highly regarded higher education institution. During the summers, undergraduate students are given the opportunity to apply to be a resident advisor (RA) for academic summer camps. Several female and male students applied for the job openings. Offers were extended to both male and female students. On average, women students simply accepted the offer, while the male students went to the Dean's Office to negotiate their summer offer. Once again, here is a great example of a lost opportunity for women (Thompson 2013). Why did the female students accept the offer at face value while their male counterparts took the time to ask questions about what was included in the offer and even requested higher pay?

These days a lot of my coaching is focused on helping young professionals not only figure out their path and net worth but also determine how and when to deploy the three negotiation tips effectively. The problem is that few of us realize the importance of improving our performance of the three tips due to our busy schedules. Normally, we do not even take the time to practice conversations with other individuals. Additionally, we might not analyze and think about another individual's perspective. We live in a low-context society where individualistic decision-making is a strong characteristic. Therefore, we might not be prone to establish rapport with a large variety of individuals. As an individualistic society, we place our decision making on ourselves instead of on a group. Since we do not think collectively, we do not take the time to figure out other people's perspective to help with relationship building and, eventually, negotiating scripted as well as unscripted scenarios.

No matter what the monetary offer is and how pleased you are with it, I always encourage my clients and mentees to ask for more. It has been my experience that employers normally do not place an offer on the table without having some cushion. This means you are going to be receiving an offer that falls short of expectations, even if you are not aware of the scale. Therefore, it is ok to ask for more. One way to do it would be by stating, "What is this job's management level and overall compensation scale?" Based on the answer received, you could follow up with, "On average, how long does it take to move up to the higher level pay scale or get promoted?" By asking these questions, you are opening the discussion to learn how the organization functions. If you are told the offer is at the highest range of the pay scale, you would be surprised how there could still be some cushion in other non-salary items, such as an extra personal day, access to an assistant, work from home one day a week, etc.

Family

Let's assume the compensation included in your offer is what you expected or even higher. It even includes non-cash driven compensation, such as extra vacation time and stock options. Now it is time to figure out how your offer complements your family piece. Even if you are single, everybody has some type of family responsibility from humans to four-legged cuties. We normally do not live in a silo without affecting other people's lives. Thus, it is imperative that with any offer being considered you ask, "How does it work with my family needs?" For example, this is the time to figure out what are the normal hours of operation at the company. Human resources might have shared the office hours; however, are they truly followed? Or, if they are followed, how much extra time is required outside of the office to get your job done? We live in a world where an eight-hour work day is unheard of. We all take work home. But is the work excessive? When I was an engineer, there was an oil company known in the community for pushing employees to work on holidays, evenings, Saturdays, and Sundays. People like myself, who felt strongly about our path, stayed away from the company. If offered a position, I simply could not be part of that business regardless of how high the salary would be.

These days, companies anticipate their employees to work 9-10+ hour days. Many times the long days include work outside the office. How can you determine if the company that offered you the job has an environment that recognizes and helps you nurture your family piece? To begin researching this information, I recommend simply asking the individuals you know in the company. If you do not know a company employee, ask your network. I bet you already know someone with connections to the company in question. Additionally, engage in the online world and see if there are any comments or discussions about the company's culture and environment. Do the same on your social media channels. Go to Twitter and follow hashtags the organization uses regularly for marketing and public relations purposes. And, last but not least, take a day in the middle of the week and check out how many cars or lights you can see after 6 p.m. at the office.

In Alexandra's case, she was in the midst of planning her wedding. Before she took the job, I encouraged her to discuss with her fiancé what life would look like if she took the job. Part of her new responsibilities would require community outreach. This called for evenings and weekend work. How would these extra hours affect their marriage? Would her husband be accepting of several weekends a year where she would be working and not at home? How would these off-hour responsibilities affect her involvement with other family members? There are no right or wrong answers to these questions. Every person has their own answers that work best for their family situation.

With an upcoming wedding, there are time requirements associated with event planning and the honeymoon. Instead of waiting until the wedding was going to take place the following year, Alexandra took the initiative to inquire about being able to take two weeks off to enjoy a honeymoon. This negotiation took place after Alexandra had her offer in hand. Before accepting it, she had the conversation of how her goal was to take longer than normal for a honeymoon. During the discussion, they addressed how the work would still be managed and completed. Although the wedding was a year away, both parties did come to an agreement, which included check-in points to allow for further evaluation.

Planning a wedding is not the only item to consider in the family piece. Instead, an individual might have other types of family responsibilities that could need some consideration from the employer. For instance, one of my clients in NYC is a strong performer at her current Fortune 100 company. She is considered a high achiever, and upper management expects a lot from her. She is in a happy relationship with her partner and their adopted children from Haiti. Her workdays are long, but she has been able to manage a work-life balance that is effective. Although she works sixty-hour weeks, she does work from home on Fridays and normally leaves work by 4:30 p.m. to get home in time for dinner. How is she able to manage such an early departure time? She arrives at work by no later than 7:30 a.m. and rarely takes a lunch hour. At home, after she puts the kids to bed, she gets back on her computer to plan her next day. In the mornings, she wakes up by 5 a.m. to get a thirty-minute workout in before she gets ready for work. Although this sounds like a very tight schedule, it works perfectly for my client. She is extremely organized. By working from home on Fridays, she is able to get in a much longer workout while diminishing her stress level before the weekend begins. She still works a 9- to 10-hour day on Friday, but does not have to deal with an afternoon commute. This way she is able to be ready for her family to begin the weekend by 5 p.m. on Friday.

You might get to a point in your negotiation where your current or future employer does not agree with any of your family needs. Although many companies are trying to incorporate work-life balance into their organizations, there are still many employers that do not implement or encourage it strongly enough. If that is your current or future employer, you need to evaluate if this is something you want to live with for the next few years. I have had some clients who have overlooked the family piece in their path in order to gain some specific experience for their resume and future career development. Although I'm not a fan of this approach, I totally understand why it needs to be considered in some instances. If this is your situation, I encourage you to identify a realistic time frame of how long you could manage this lifestyle followed with the necessary steps and tactics for an exit strategy. I will guarantee a burnout for any individual who will work extremely long hours for extended periods of time with no real balance.

Interest

The last piece of your path is normally the one that is least considered and addressed. We live in a society where we all strive to do our best at work while fully associating ourselves with what we do for a living. Therefore, hobbies and outside interests have taken a backseat for most of us throughout our careers. Our work is demanding fifty-hour workweeks and any free time is devoted to our family responsibilities. Add to it any commuting time, and we are left with minimum free time for our interests.

As human beings we can certainly survive without nurturing our hobbies. But only imagine how much fun and fulfilling your life could be if you allocated some "me-time." Research studies have shown how taking care of one's self is essential. Even when you are on a plane, the flight attendant will state to place your oxygen mask on yourself before you help others. That statement needs to be taken seriously by all of us. What do we need to do for us before we take care of others? Or before we take care of our jobs?

Assuming the job could totally fulfill this need is not realistic. I have come across some clients whose interests are closely correlated to their work. However, they do not only rely on their employer to fulfill all of their interests. They have tapped into other ways to nourish their needs. I currently sit on a board that provides guidance to a local non-profit organization focused on empowering young female students. Our board treasurer happens to be a financial advisor in a large firm. He truly enjoys working with numbers and any spreadsheets related to Profit & Loss (P&L), balance sheets and cash flow statements. It is amazing the amount of creativity this individual brings to the board. By allowing his financial expertise to shine in our board meetings, he is also able to lead excellent discussions around strategy and marketing topics. He has even stated how fun it is to be able to not only manage the numbers but also really work on determining how we improve the other functions in the organization based on the financials. As a financial advisor for a large investment firm, he is not given the opportunity to get involved in strategic and long-term marketing discussions. His focus is solely finances. Although he offers suggestions to his direct supervisor, he feels that his ideas are not shared with upper management. They simply stop at his supervisor's level. By serving on this board, he is able to fulfill an item in his interest piece.

Many of us might not be interested or have the opportunity of serving on a board. Some of us might be interested in volunteering our services and time to causes dear to our heart. Take, for instance, my client Marianne. Since a young age she became very interested in Habitat for Humanity. During her college years, she had the opportunity to meet President Jimmy Carter in one of Habitat for Humanity's projects in the state of Georgia. She was so impressed with the effort that she made it a point to take vacation time to volunteer. As she evolved in her career, it became obvious that taking time off to volunteer was becoming more difficult. She was a single mom, and any vacation or personal days were dedicated to her child and not volunteering efforts. During her last promotion review she took the risk and asked for it. She had been offered the position of vice president of business development for a technology company. Her compensation as well as family needs were fully taken care of by the offer. She had been part of the company for the past four years, and her track record was second to none. When discussing the offer, she expressed to her supervisor how important it was to be involved in the community. She shared how she had improved her leadership skills in her current position but also through her volunteering experiences over the past several years. Fortunately, Habitat for Humanity has a strong presence in the community she lives. Every year there is at least one Habitat for Humanity project taking place in her area. During her negotiation, she was able to illustrate the importance of her volunteering time and how it helps her as a manager and leader. This discussion took multiple sessions, but in the end she was able to negotiate two extra paid days off from work that would allow her to be part of a Habitat for Humanity project. These extra days did not affect her vacation time.

Marianne was able to secure this deal since the organization's president also volunteers in the local community and public relations efforts are done in conjunction with his service. Most of her coworkers and friends also volunteer. Therefore, asking for volunteering time as part of her interest was a win-win for the organization. This illustrates how really knowing your interest is essential for your own success. If you have a strong interest in volunteering, you can deploy the three tips of prepare, practice, and perspective to determine if the organization you are targeting makes sense for you. Take the time to prepare by inquiring and doing research on how the organization's president and other leaders feel about your interest. Do they encourage volunteering? Do they do it themselves? If the answers are yes, then prepare yourself to have the conversation on how you would like to fulfill your volunteering needs. Develop the script and practice it with a mentor, coach, or friend. Get used to saying the necessary words and asking for it like Marianne did. She practiced how to manage an answer of "no" or "maybe" from her direct supervisor. She got to the point where she was not discouraged listening to a negative response. She took the time to reframe her offer until her direct supervisor saw the value of her volunteering. By practicing so much, Marianne understood that everybody had a different perspective. Although her president and the management team volunteered on an annual basis, none of them had ever gotten involved with Habitat for Humanity. Their volunteering was focused toward shelters and food banks during the holiday season. One of Marianne's reframing approaches was illustrating how she could "hold down the fort" during the senior management team's outings to food banks to serve lunches around the holiday season. Meanwhile, she will be gone for two days during the summer months when nobody in the leadership team takes time off to fulfill his or her volunteer interests.

Your interest piece is not simply correlated to volunteering. Similar to the family piece, interest has to do with what you need as an individual to help you reach your goal in developing as a professional. For instance, in Alexandra's case, her interest lies in getting involved in community outreach and leadership while enjoying her love for music and local talent. Her job does offer her an avenue to develop the first two elements, but she also has other outlets to tap into if her job cannot fulfill her interests regularly. Negotiating professional development could be a venue for Alexandra to consider. She could have the opportunity to participate in a local multi-month leadership program for millennials interested in making a difference in the legislation, education, and healthcare fields. This topic was discussed during her job offer time frame. Although no formal agreement was reached at the time, her supervisor did agree to have the conversation once again during her six-

and twelve-month evaluations. This level of commitment from her supervisor illustrates the capability of being able to negotiate something that could be beneficial to both. It will be Alexandra's responsibility to ensure the topic is discussed during the pre-agreed time frames.

Another interest might be related to continued education. How many of us have asked if an organization is willing to provide monetary assistance for pursuing a graduate degree? I assume not very many. Recently, I spoke with a colleague who has been involved in getting her PhD in education. It has been a very long road. On several occasions she has felt defeated and tired with the process. She is currently writing her dissertation. She shared her progress with her organization's president and, to her surprise, the president asked her when would be the best time to take a sabbatical in order to complete her education. My colleague almost fainted when she heard those words. She never thought about this alternative. However, the organization's president has an advanced degree and spends a good amount of her work time interfacing with education-driven institutions and efforts. Additionally, the president does not want to lose an employee who is a valued asset to the company. The president also realizes my colleague is at a point in her career where leaving the organization might be necessary in order to continue growing as a leader. When my colleague shared the news with me, I encouraged her to put together a sabbatical plan that identifies timelines and ways that her responsibilities will be accomplished during her paid time off. The organization is providing my colleague with an excellent way to help her achieve one of her long-term goals: earning a PhD. Therefore, my colleague needs to illustrate how it is a win-win situation for all parties involved.

It is easy to get swept off your feet when an offer comes in and to say yes automatically. This chapter teaches us that it is best to take a few days and really see if the offer is in line with our path. If, by any chance, the offer does not complement your path, it is time to negotiate. Sometimes an offer may come in that does not have all that you desire at the onset, but that does not mean you cannot negotiate to make it work for you.

CHAPTER 6

ENSURE YOUR SUCCESS IN NINETY DAYS

You worked very hard to land the job. It seems as if you spent so much time simply negotiating everything. You are set to begin your new position in two weeks. You are excited and feel invincible. Do not get too used to it because reality will sink in quite quickly. Max Messmer, chairman of Accountemps and author of *Human Resources Kit For Dummies®*, said it best, "The first few days and weeks on a job can be both exciting and overwhelming as new hires familiarize themselves with the company's work environment and policies, including any unwritten rules" (Brooks 2012). This is also when it is easiest to forget about your path because you want to impress those you work with. During the first ninety days of employment, it is important to ensure you are staying true to your long-term goals and also learning whether the organization is an environment or place for you to truly reach them. To address this effectively, focus on sticking to your list and learning the organization's politics.

Stick to Your List

One of my clients, a Latina working in higher education, held an administrative position at a prestigious research university. For purposes of this book, let's call her Susan. She had negotiated her job to perfection. Not only was she receiving higher compensation than she expected, but she also was able to transfer her tenure status. She was the highest-ranking Latina at the university. By the time she began her job, she was known across campus and was invited to every event related to women and Latinas. Her calendar was bursting with invitations. The level of interest from not only faculty but also students and staff overwhelmed her. She immediately realized this position was not about her, it was about every Latina and woman currently associated with the university, as well as any Latinas and women in higher education. She admitted that when she was negotiating the position she had never taken into account this type of work-driven social activity.

Susan's list of to-dos grew longer on a daily basis. Soon, she was working 12- to 13-hour days and trying to do the best she could on campus. For the past decade, I had coached her on time management and overall negotiation skills. She knew the importance of getting some easy wins under her belt during the first ninety days on the job. Due to her growing list of tasks, plus the overwhelming requests of her time, she decided to focus on time management to ensure the best utilization of her working hours. She knew the importance of taking into account the three main pieces (career, family, and interest) in her path. Susan had incorporated them during her job negotiation, and she knew it was important to keep them very present as she navigated her new position.

Unfortunately, Susan's time was limited and she began cutting corners. With the new position she had fulfilled the career piece to the best of her abilities. During the job negotiation, she was very straightforward about the importance of her family and interest pieces. She even had multiple conversations with her soon-to-be direct supervisor and the human resources vice president about her needs when it came to family and interests. Her family piece included having dinner with her family three nights a week. Her interest piece included practicing yoga once or twice during the workweek and once over the weekend.

Planning is really not effective unless you are able to execute correctly. Susan had planned perfectly, but within the first ninety days on the job she realized the execution aspect of it was not working. She had overcommitted and now was trying to figure out how to regain control. Why should Susan care so much about her performance during the first ninety days on the job? Michael D. Watkins, co-founder of leadership development company Genesis Advisers and author of *"The First 90 Days: Proven Strategies for Getting Up to Speed Faster and Smarter,"* says, "My research shows that what you do early on during a job transition is what matters most. Your colleagues and your boss form opinions about you based on limited information, and those opinions are sticky–it's hard to change their minds. So shape their impressions of you to the best of your ability." (Bianchi 2014). By not being able to balance career, family, and interests effectively during the first ninety days, Susan was illustrating that her main and only focus was to work. Although she knew she was going to be working long days, she never expected for 12- to 13-hour days to become the norm. Simply, she had overcommitted herself. She had a huge list of responsibilities and a longer list of requests to speak and mentor the women in the university. Susan was a people person and truly found satisfaction from spending one-on-one and group time with the women on campus. However, she found herself on a daily basis not only performing her job but also spending a couple of hours mentoring, speaking, and engaging with other women across campus. We have all heard the term "Monday morning quarterbacking," where it becomes very obvious what you are doing wrong the day after. When Susan and I spoke, she did expect for the conversation to become a Monday morning quarterbacking session. Actually, she went there before I could. She knew what she was doing wrong, but it seemed she could not stop the madness. Her call to me was her way to communicate that she needed an intervention.

Any professional can easily fall into Susan's despair. As a coach, I encourage clients who find themselves in positions similar to Susan's to establish and implement a checklist to follow once they have found and started a position that complements their path. Susan knew what she wanted and needed to succeed. She started her job and immediately developed a checklist. However, this list was one-sided; it only included the career piece. Susan thought the other two pieces would simply be included, since she discussed them at length during the interview process. One thing Susan did not realize was that simply discussing it with your future boss is not enough. Making another person aware of your needs and wants does not guarantee your ability to implement your desire effectively. Yes, her boss knew about the family dinners and yoga time; however, it really was not her supervisor's task to ensure such desires were fulfilled. Instead, it is Susan's responsibility to track and measure her own checklist. When Susan and I sat down for a coaching session, we discussed the items that should have been included on the list. For starters, it needs to be utilized as a measurement device of the three-piece categories of a person's path. Additionally, the list needs to be simple and short to ensure proper implementation. The more that is placed on the list, the harder it will be to abide by it. For Susan's case her checklist would have looked as follows.

INGREDIENT TYPE	ACTIVITY	CHECK COMPLETE
Career	• During the first ninety days, establish meetings with peers, subordinates, and supervisors to identify their expectations of you. • Once the ninety days have passed, revisit with the same individuals to measure your performance and identify their expectations for the first year. • Develop a to-do list with time frames to revisit on a weekly basis with your direct supervisor. • Develop an alliance list of individuals you can help and who can help you across the institute. • Define when and how you will meet and further develop a relationship. These alliances need to be categorized into three groups: operations, strategic and professional/political development.	

Career	• Develop and implement a monthly speaking calendar that has you participating in three to five events on a monthly basis. • Identify one to two people to mentor and conduct meetings mainly over the phone and via email. • Develop and implement a networking schedule that has you attending one event every two weeks.	
Family	• Have dinner with family 3 evenings per week • Identify and communicate number of vacations and time off for the next year • Identify one day a week to be on campus for no more than 8 hours in order to get home on time • Identify 2 days a month to work from home to avoid commuting time.	

Interest	• Attend yoga class over the weekend	
	• Attend yoga class at university once a week	
	• Attend yoga class near my home once a week	
	• Identify a way to decompress on a daily basis	

This is not an exhaustive list. It just provides a quick idea of the items that can be included in a checklist. Every person will have a different list and needs to monitor it on a weekly basis. I normally recommend referring to the list on a daily basis during the first ninety days on the job to ensure proper deployment. Once your checklist is effectively deployed, it is time to focus on learning the rules of the organization. Learning the politics of your work environment can help you see what aspects of your path may or may not be achieved.

Learn the Politics

Sounds simple, doesn't it? But we all know that it is far more complicated. In any job, especially at the beginning, a person is learning all the time. However, in this case, I am referring to taking the time to really learn about the politics and the unwritten rules of the organization. When somebody starts a job, there is normally a human resources training where individuals hear about the benefits, standard operating procedures, and anything else associated with the organization. Like in any family, an organization also has the unwritten rules that people follow without discussing with others. For instance, do people take their lunch hour to run errands or is this a department where going out for lunch, no matter the reason, is frowned upon?

During one of my management positions in a consumer products company, I was surprised to learn the importance of showing the chief financial officer (CFO) and other C-level executives how hard you worked by eating breakfast and lunch at your desk. Within my first week on the job, I learned the importance of setting my alarm for 5 a.m. to arrive at work before 6 a.m. so I could work out in their state-of-the-art gym and then be in my office by 7:30 a.m. with a coffee and bagel in hand. I was amazed to realize how meetings were scheduled between 7:30 a.m. and 6 p.m. My daily calendar needed to be available for meetings for almost eleven hours. Additionally, I never left the building before the CFO. It was his practice to pass by every office during his way out. This activity would take place normally around 6:45 p.m. Although I broached the subject about work-life balance during the interview process, I was never told about these rules. Instead, we talked about the state-of-the-art gym and the healthy menu items offered in the cafeteria, both of which were right in line with my family and interest pieces. I made the wrong assumption. I should have asked some clarifying questions concerning these topics. Is the gym opened during the evening hours or weekends? Could my husband join me? Why is the cafeteria opened for eighteen hours a day? What type of extracurricular activities do employees engage in? Do we have a shift-driven workplace? By asking these questions, I could have gained a better perspective on the company's environment, which would have allowed me to make a better determination if this was the right place for me to work. I was now an employee and realized trying to negotiate fewer working hours was not an option in this type of environment. Although I prospered during my tenure at this company, I eventually left to find an opportunity with better work-life balance. My next employer did have a gym, and I learned from my questions that the employees and their families used it over the weekends and during the evening hours. These answers showed an environment that would allow me to fulfill my family and interest pieces as well as career.

It is possible that in the first ninety days you realize the job you took is not going to check off all the pieces of your path. It even might take you away from a lot of them. When this happens, it is up to you to decide whether to stay with it or opt for another opportunity.

The first ninety days on the job can be stressful, but it is within these days that you will know if this is the right environment for you. You will also establish your reputation as a performer and individual. You must stay focused on your long-term goals. It is normal to overcommit to tasks and responsibilities. This way you are able to demonstrate your strengths and capabilities to your supervisors, colleagues, and team. However, make certain you are not neglecting what is truly important to you.

CHAPTER 7

THREE STEPS TO BEAT CONFLICT

You have been on the job for a month, a year, or even longer. You still feel, no matter how hard you work, you are always scaling a mountain trying to negotiate your path. It seems as if you are battling or compromising to get what you need. How do you manage that uncomfortable feeling and state that comes with disagreement and conflict? Creating the right environment for your path and long-term goals is not always going to be easy, and you will come up against a lot of pushback. Hence, how do you deal with the situation when your boss says he or she will not let you attend the leadership conference you had discussed during the interview process? Instead of just being disappointed and complaining to others about the situation, it is imperative that you acknowledge and articulate your concerns and feelings, deploy active listening skills, and reflect on a solution or alternative. Deploying these three approaches can move you toward being viewed as a strong professional capable of having difficult conversations and getting things done.

Acknowledge and Articulate Your Concerns and Feelings

As an Alternative Dispute Resolution (ADR) strategist, I am amazed by how many professionals view solving conflict as something that can be managed without any feelings. They believe if the feelings are suppressed or avoided, it would be easier to simply survive. From my experience as a workplace conflict mediator, I say it is all the opposite. When any disagreement arises between individuals, it is human nature to experience a variety of feelings; from frustration and defeat to anger and fatigue.

It is normal to feel defeated when your direct supervisor responds with a "no" to one of your path's interests like continued education, for example. When receiving this type of negative feedback, it is important that you acknowledge and understand the feelings you are experiencing. How could a short word like "no" create such huge disappointment, frustration, and anger? As a mediator, I normally see these types of feelings in any disagreement. No matter the circumstances, receiving a negative response to your request is not something easy to manage. Therefore, you need to be ready to learn how to manage your reaction by acknowledging and articulating your concerns and feelings about the rejection.

It is fine to acknowledge to the other person that you are frustrated or tired or simply disappointed with the situation. Obviously, be respectful when you are sharing such feelings. Do not bash the other party and claim they are not holding up their end of the bargain. Instead, admit and accept this is not going to be easy. Therefore, I recommend using the "I message" tool when having to share a difficult message. Not only are you delivering the message from your perspective without judging the other person but you are also infusing an environment of factual sharing rather than critique. To do this, simply follow this formula, which I learned at The Conflict Center in Denver:

- Start your communication by stating: I think we are not on the same page, or I believe we may have a misunderstanding from what we discussed
- Provide a reason for your statement: Because (state the problem in one sentence)
- Conclude with a joint effort approach: Therefore, I recommend we (state a solution in one or two sentences)

A key factor about this formula is the exclusion of using the word "you". Instead use "I", "we," or "us". This forces you to be fully inclusive and take ownership of the situation. Additionally, it shows that you are providing information rather than judging the other party. It also helps you show respect and willingness to listen to other options. This formula is very much utilized by mediators and coaches when guiding a conversation with their clients. I have had several caucuses where I asked the party to develop his or her "I message." Prior to going back to the mediator table and sharing it with the other party, I have them practice their "I message" with me. I want to make sure they feel comfortable stating and listening to the words and message.

Recently, I was mediating a high-profile performance evaluation workplace case. The party had been accused of mismanaging funds during the past year. Allegedly, there was proof of this mismanagement. When I first took the case, I thought it was an easy one. I expected it to take only a couple of hours to mediate. Instead, it took more than six sessions to discuss and reach an agreement. Throughout every session, I spent time talking with each side at caucus and trying to figure out how to get them to communicate better to identify the true problem. One of the biggest hurdles was their communication style. The millennial employee was open, approachable, and collaborative and expected to be involved in most decisions. The superior was a non-accommodating baby boomer who believed decision-making opportunities were earned after several years of hard work and commitment. As you can imagine, the feelings escalated immediately. Whatever one party said, the other would answer with a "no." There was not a session where voices were not raised and insults were not shared among the parties.

As a true believer of acknowledging and sharing your concerns and feelings, I knew I could not let this type of behavior just foster along. I had to provide the parties with the tools to let them share their feelings while being respectful toward each other. When I first introduced the "I message" tool, both parties thought I was nuts. As the mediator, I simply requested for them to try it as we progressed discussing the different items on the list. At first, the deployment of the tool felt unnatural and even forced. However, as I kept on caucusing with each party individually on this topic, I soon noticed a shift in the discussion at the mediation table. No longer did we hear raised voices or even punches on the table when a "no" was shared. Instead, we were listening to words and messages that were strong and difficult but were delivered in a respectful manner.

By shifting your communication, you are capable of getting the conversation back on the right track. Your boss may not change his or her mind at this time concerning your continued education request. Nevertheless, by having a civil communication you are able to illustrate the importance of your request. You have the opportunity to reiterate your path, and how it is an important tool to ensure your and your company's success.

Similar to receiving a response of "no" from your boss, imagine dealing with a highly competitive colleague whose main goal is to win at all costs. This means he or she has his or her own agenda and does not take the time or simply care about others. The person strongly believes his or her knowledge and expertise cannot be matched by anybody. I spent over fifteen years in the managerial ranks of corporate

America surrounded by these types of individuals. I even became one as a survival mechanism. You do not need to be in corporate America to experience these types of individuals. In today's competitive field everybody is just focusing on their own goals and overall success. I know I have stated the importance of having and deploying your own path; however, it is essential that you communicate yours with others and work together to determine how your and everybody's path can be respected and considered. When you are part of a team at work or in your personal life, it is not just about your path. It is about acknowledging, understanding, and articulating everybody's agreements, disagreement, fears, and concerns. Additionally, it is about how everybody's path pieces are managed for the success of the team as a whole and not for the success of one individual.

Recently, some of my clients have extended their coaching engagements due to situations where they cannot effectively manage the implementation of their path. One of my clients even had a written agreement from her soon-to-be boss about how she was going to manage family and interests in a high-power position. The written agreement was gained electronically. My client outlined in an email the agreed upon items discussed during a meeting, and her future boss responded in agreement electronically. It took less than a month for my client to begin struggling with the implementation. Immediately, she became frustrated and confused. Not only did she receive an agreement from her supervisor but she also had taken the time to reach out to her colleagues and share her goals and inquire about theirs. Her intent was to begin the conversation on how to incorporate everybody's needs. These discussions were well-received. Unfortunately, the topic derailed quite quickly when two of her colleagues pulled work tenure on her regarding weekend work. One of my client's interests was to spend as many weekends as possible with her family, while preparing to participate in a half-marathon. She knew this job required some weekend work attending community gatherings; however, during her conversations, it became very clear that everybody shared this task equally. When the first work weekend came around, all of her colleagues pointed to her as the person to take care of the work. She was the "new kid on the block," plus it was a weekend forecasted to be warm and sunny. People just wanted to have fun outside and not work! My client was not only furious with her colleagues' reactions, she also was very disappointed and sad. She felt too emotional to even speak. When she and I spoke, she shared how she felt that the time she put into planning and updating her path was just dismissed.

I understand why her colleagues wanted her to be the individual to work the weekend. After all, they had been covering weekend work for the past year and half, and she had just started the job. Although they understood my client's interest piece, I can only imagine they felt that she needed to "put in her time" before her interests could have equal weight to theirs. I actually agreed with her colleagues' viewpoint. As the new person on the job, many times you need to put in extra time in the career piece and sacrifice some of the family and interest pieces. However, when you take such an approach, you need to be clear with others on what you are doing. Use the "I message" tool to communicate such information. In my client's case, she could have stated: "I can see why you think I should be working this weekend because I'm the new person on the job. I know it will give me the necessary exposure and experience I need to start establishing my credibility in the market. However, I recommend we, as a team, discuss a realistic calendar that identifies everybody's weekend work responsibility while taking into account our personal interests." It is important when you are working as a team to take the time to share and listen to everybody's feelings on how to manage all of the path's pieces. This is not about who wins or who loses. This is about keeping it real while allowing for everybody to effectively manage their needs. This requires sharing your true feelings while intently listening to and engaging in other's feelings and thoughts. When sharing your thoughts, be respectful of all the parties involved and focus your information-sharing on how you see it without pointing fingers, judging, or demeaning others. Take the time to develop the necessary "I messages" when the going gets tough.

Active Listening

Active listening is the hardest trait to deploy effectively. We all think we are great at listening. However, as human beings we tend to prefer to talk rather than listen. This is especially present in a low-context culture society like the one in the United States. Low-context is defined as a culture where people do not really know or seem to share all of the same values or history as others do. A country of immigrants like ours tends to gravitate to this type of society. Let me start by saying this is not a bad thing. It is simply an individualistic society where direct, casual approach communication takes place with a low tolerance for silence and a high tolerance for questions. Decisions are sought out by providing precise and very technical information that might be delivered bluntly, causing opposing opinions. In addition, we thrive as a nation where everybody can state their opinion and thoughts via a variety of platforms. This type of society might tend to reward individuals with a more competitive style.

The intent here is not to say that receiving a "no" from your boss is the end of the world. All the opposite, a "no" can generate new ways and ideas on how to progress and deal with a situation. In recent years, we have become a society of wanting everything immediately. Plus, we are vocal and competitive about demanding what we want. It seems that if your boss rejects your ideas, you cannot have a lively, respectful conversation where everybody involved can politely disagree while learning from each other's differences. Yes, it is hurtful to be on the receiving end of a "no" answer, especially if it comes from somebody with authority. You are entitled to feel that way, but you need to acknowledge that the other party's decision might have a larger reason behind it. It would be great if we could just discuss and learn from each other. As a coach, I have spent endless hours practicing active listening techniques with my clients, many of which I learned during a Spring Institute training in Denver in the fall of 2005. Identifying the path is fun and invigorating; however, we must be ready to manage the disagreements that might be generated from our path.

Receiving a negative response from your boss is not the end of the world. Instead, consider it to be a learning moment.

How and what can you learn from the situation? A lot. But to be able to learn, you need to deploy active listening skills to control your emotions. By deploying these types of skills, you are able to act more as a reporter. By doing so, you gain more information about why the negative decision was made and how you can identify other options for the long-term.

You can Google active listening and a huge amount of information emerges. Based on all the information offered, I recommend using the following five steps to ensure proper deployment of active listening.

Level 1 – Basic Acknowledgement

Take the time to let the other party know you are listening. This can be done in multiple ways:

- Non-verbal (head nodding, leaning forward, etc.)
- Verbal responses (really, interesting, uh- huh, etc.).

Level 2 – Silence

When engaged in a conversation, remember the correlation between how many ears and mouth you have on your head. Use that correlation to determine how much time you should spend speaking and how much time you should spend listening. This is easier said than done. Experts have shown how individuals gather more information when they listen than when they speak. This is a technique used by mediators all the time. It is amazing what a person will share with you when you are listening to him or her.

Level 3 – Questions

When you take the time to ask questions, you are showing the other party your interest level. It also tells the other party you want to know more. By asking questions you increase your understanding of the other party's needs and wants. It makes the other person feel as if you really care. Therefore, he or she might put more effort in sharing important information with you.

Level 4 – Paraphrasing

According to dictionary.com, paraphrasing is defined as "a restatement of a text or passage giving the meaning in another form, as for clearness; rewording." This step focuses on content and involves interpreting what you think the speaker said, then getting verification that you are correct.

Level 5 – Reflective Listening

Based on wikipedia.org, reflective listening is a communication strategy involving two key steps: seeking to understand a speaker's idea, then offering the idea back to the speaker to confirm the idea has been understood correctly. By deploying reflective listening, you are truly engaging in the conversation. You are able to help the other party and yourself filter through the message content, while setting aside emotions.

When you deploy these five active listening steps, you are able to better understand the dynamics of a negative response. When we receive a "no" answer from a superior, it does not feel right, and it is not welcomed. You must realize that a decision always takes a lot of things into consideration. Active listening skills will help you better understand what they are, and then guide you on how to alter your own path. At this point, you need to reflect on alternatives so you and your boss can identify a solution that will work in the short and long terms.

Reflect on a Solution or an Alternative

You have taken the time to embrace your as well as the other party's feelings. You have deployed multiple "I messages" and active listening tools throughout your conversation. However, you are about to reach a solution or alternative and something happens where discussions break down. You hear another "no" out of your boss' mouth. What happened? Or better yet, why did this happen? Normally, this is very present in any situation where all involved have been rushed to a decision or simply feel like not committing at this point. When was the last time you were invested in something but at the end you decided to pullout and not commit? This could happen to your boss. Yes, he or she heard you and agreed with your path when you were hired. Then outside issues, such as the market, a funder, or even inside concerns, a bad performer, a recent departure, may have caused a change in direction and focus. This happened to me when I entered the telecommunications field. I was changing functions as well as industries. Therefore, I took the time to update my path to illustrate a more realistic approach to my pieces. To ensure a short learning curve, I took it upon myself to place a stronger focus on career over the other two pieces. My career focus included long workdays and significant travel to get to know the team across the country. The day my boss denied my travel to one of my regions due to budget constraints and a travel freeze, I almost lost my calm. He and I had discussed the importance of my getting on the road immediately and ensuring every month I spent at least 50 percent of my time visiting our field offices. By denying my request to spend a week in the Pacific Northwest visiting ten field offices, he just gave me the message that I was not valued. I viewed this rejection as a slap on my face after the commitment I had made to the organization during my hiring process. We had discussed in length how I was going to sacrifice my family and interest time to ensure I could deliver immediate positive results.

The good news was that I was able to control my outburst by acknowledging my fears and concerns using "I messages" and active listening techniques. For starters, I remember using the following "I message" the second I was hit by the negative news. I stated to my boss, "I feel very frustrated because we discussed visiting our field offices was imperative for the success of this group. Therefore, I recommend we talk about this further tomorrow when I have some more time to reflect on the news." Instead, I could have said, "This is ridiculous! You promised me I could travel. Now with a freeze on the travel budget I won't be able to excel and it will be your fault if I don't perform to your high standards, which will result in a very small bonus and pay raises for me in the future." Imagine being my boss and hearing the latter communication. I bet you would not be happy or willing to have a reasonable conversation with me. That is the purpose of the "I message." You can still communicate your frustration, but it must be in a more factual approach rather than an emotional one. By controlling your accusatory tone, you are able to get the other party to understand there is a need for further discussion.

No matter your work environment and the news received, you must take the time to reflect on the situation at hand. For me, not being able to travel to a field office translated into delaying a promotion opportunity. I was determined to learn everything about the business during my first six months of employment. Now that business travel was being controlled, it would not allow me to establish the necessary relationships with the field office personnel while learning about the nuts and bolts of the business. Usually, we do not take the time to reflect and assess much about a decision. We basically react and make assumptions that might be wrong, and our behavior could affect the future of our career in the organization. Therefore, take the time to determine what needs immediate attention versus what needs more long-term focus. This is called reflecting time. You have your own time frame for how things need to evolve at work. However, you need to be prepared to receive and analyze any negative news. It is time for you to share your thoughts and concerns with your direct supervisor. Get his or her input on what could be done to keep you on track when it comes to learning the business and getting exposed to the necessary people. Do not just come to a conclusion without asking yourself the following reflective questions.

- Will this change make a difference in three months, six months, or one year?
- Could we as an organization or individual benefit from anything different that might evolve from this limitation or change?
- How will the changes affect my role? Do I feel comfortable with it?

I recommend you reach out to a buddy, mentor, and/or friend to have the conversation about your answers. Ask them to help you answer the questions by taking into account their perspective. Basically, take a deep breath and think before you act. This recommendation is very valuable for everything in life. On most occasions, we do not need to react or make a decision immediately. We can take some time to do nothing and simply process the information we have heard.

Therefore, no matter the issue, ensure to acknowledge the people and circumstances affecting the situation. Then focus on deploying active listening skills as you hear the information. And finally, before you make a decision, reflect on what you have heard. Take the time to absorb your learnings and feelings. We know you need to make decisions and reach an end point, but adding some extra time to the process will help you in the long run. You will reach the final point in a happier and less stressed state.

CHAPTER 8
MAKE YOUR OWN DIFFERENCE

I have had the fortune of coaching and mentoring several women throughout my career. No matter their backgrounds, skill levels, or viewpoints, they all deal with similar concerns and issues. These issues can all be managed if they take the time to figure out their net worth. Interestingly enough, when I state net worth to them they think I am referring to a monetary topic. But by now, you should have realized it is not just about money. It is about identifying and balancing the key pieces needed to have a fulfilling life and existence. By doing this, you are able to manage your path in the long-term. Basically, whoever said, "Money can't buy you happiness" hit the nail right on the head. I have coached and worked with multiple individuals whose primary focus was money. I have learned very quickly from working with them that money really did not materialize into what they were seeking.

One of my coaching clients was a strong-willed, professionally driven woman that was hungry for power. When we first met, she stated the importance of making money and having power since she grew up poor with no good access to education, health, and entertainment. She had been working since the age of fourteen to help her family. She knew her only way out was education. She spent her teenage years working, studying, and focusing on getting a scholarship to attend college. After graduating with a degree in math, she entered the business world. She worked her way up to a vice president position before her thirtieth birthday. By the time we met, she was in her late thirties and heading a very large marketing agency on the West Coast. By all standards, she had made it! She had obtained everything she had sought out: the title, the position, the car, the home overlooking the beach, the partner, the blended family, the pets, the network of friends, you name it. However, she reached a point where she felt unfulfilled and somewhat frustrated with herself as a human being.

During our first few talks, it became very clear that my client was a perfect example of how to succeed in business. Nevertheless, she was not happy. There was something missing. My client had worked so hard to improve her life as well as her parents' and siblings'. Her focus was about working hard and succeeding. She was the top performer, the person that led community efforts, and the family member that took care of everybody in need. However, at the tender young age of thirty-eight, she found herself questioning if she had taken the right path.

We spent the following coaching sessions talking about her path. She had not heard that terminology before. She was surprised that something as simple as managing three pieces (career, family, and interests) effectively can generate a net worth that is sought out by so many of us. During our conversations, it was very easy to discuss her goals and objectives when it came to her career and family pieces. Those pieces were very present since her upbringing. Therefore, managing them long-term was an easy task. However, when we began discussing her interests piece, she stumbled and inquired what should be included in it. We began the talk with what she loved to do for fun. For my client, this topic was difficult to address. She had never had the luxury of free time since her youth. Every moment was taken up studying or working. After multiple discussions, my client realized she had never given herself the room to think about her interests.

With my guidance, my client took the time to identify two to four activities she would enjoy and that would fulfill her as an individual. These activities were not related to her family members or her business world. To begin, she admitted her love for the fine arts, where she always dreamt about being a painter. She began taking painting classes. She also realized that even though she had been a healthy eater all her life, she really never took an interest in a physical activity where she could relieve any stress. And finally, she identified that her network of individuals were work-related as well as family members. She really had never developed friendships. She was a thirty-eight-year-old woman identifying places and venues to get to know individuals who were not related to her work or family.

After working together, my client was able to create the life that made her feel accomplished, successful, and happy. Instead of just focusing on business bottom lines and worrying about family issues, she ensured to identify, implement, and sustain her balanced path.

My wish for you is that you too are able to negotiate your way to a better life. I want you to be able to take the time to focus on creating and implementing your own path. When you are managing your path, you must be ready to negotiate the key pieces: career, family, and interests. If I, as well as my clients, have been able to go from being stressed and impatient with life to a fulfilled, successful professional, I know you can do it too.

You can make your own difference!

REFERENCES

Babcock, Linda, and Sara Laschever. 2003. *Women Don't Ask: Negotiation and the Gender Divide.* Princeton: Princeton University Press. Kindle edition.

Bianchi, Jane. 2014. "The First 90 Days: Secrets to Succeeding at a New Job." *LearnVest.* June 10. https://www.learnvest.com/2014/06/new-job-success/

Brooks, Chad. 2012. "7 Tips for Starting Off a New Job on the Right Foot." *Business News Daily.* December 14. http://www.businessnewsdaily.com/3591-new-job-tips.html

Diamond, Stuart. 2012. *Getting More: How You Can Negotiate to Succeed in Work and Life.* New York: Crown Business.

Nin, Anaïs. 1961. *Seduction of the Minatour.* Chicago: The Swallow Press.

Thompson, Leigh. *"Negotiation Theory and Research: Gender and Race."* 2013. YouTube video, 1:26:29. Posted by Kellogg School of Management, April 5, https://www.youtube.com/watch?v=2aHtwLEg8R4

ACKNOWLEDGEMENTS

I can't believe I have finished my first book. Although I am the author, there are a lot of people behind the scenes who have been instrumental in supporting me along the way so I could accomplish this goal.

I would like to thank my attentive husband and helpful daughter, who just left me alone when I needed to focus on writing and editing. They encouraged me during the entire journey. Both of them are quite introspective and kindly provided valuable insight on the theme. I have learned so much from both of them!

I would like to express my gratitude to several individuals who helped me create this book. From my dear mentees Shadia Lemus, Erika Reyes Martinez and Alexandra Alonso to my dear friend Liz Antry and my business colleague Suzanne Sable, I thank you all for your time and support.

You have always believed in me and encouraged me to "just do it." You took the time to discuss the message with me, offer comments, proofread and assist with editing. If I ever find myself in need to survive, then you are the individuals I would enlist in my winning team.

Also, sincere thanks to The Author Incubator Program for steering me through this process and making me accountable for finishing my book.

And last, but not least: I want to thank my wonderful mother (*mami*), Consuelo Elizabeth Suárez, who is no longer with us. My *mami* dedicated her lifetime to providing me with direction, offering her insight, and constantly reinforcing her love, all while guiding me to be the person that I am today. I am especially grateful that she taught me to have a sense of balance in my life.

ABOUT THE AUTHOR

Author's photo courtesy of John S. Miller Photography

E lizabeth Suárez is an accomplished practitioner, management consultant, and expert in Alternative Dispute Resolution and Leadership. With more than fifteen years spent climbing the ranks of corporate America, Elizabeth insists, "Current phraseology imposes a change in our accountability," as she too further broadened her knowledge base and sharpened her negotiation skillset. Today, Elizabeth is highly regarded as an author, speaker, facilitator, coach, strategist, trainer, and mediator. Most importantly, Elizabeth researched, studied, and understands millennials, generation Y, generation X and baby boomers, and has created a platform to effectively work with them. She is passionate about imparting professionals and assisting all generations and communities to better understand how to manage disagreements, succeed in any negotiation, and develop the necessary strategies and tactics for success, all while deploying ethical persuasion and inclusiveness skills.

As a bicultural and bilingual strategist, Elizabeth is an expert in providing an amicable environment where difficult issues can be successfully addressed and resolved. Currently, Elizabeth works with clients in the fields of higher education, government, business and non-profit.

Elizabeth holds an MBA from The Wharton School of Business, University of Pennsylvania and a BS in chemical engineering from Cornell University. She completed the Executive Management Program at the John F. Kennedy School of Government at Harvard University. She is a graduate of the prestigious National Hispana Leadership Institute (NHLI) program, as well as the Center for Creative Leadership in Denver. She received her mediation training from the Colorado Council of Mediators and the Colorado Bar Association. In addition, Elizabeth is a certified MBTI practitioner. To pay it forward, Elizabeth spent many years mentoring Latina professionals and serving on the boards of multiple non-profit organizations. She lives in Colorado with her husband and daughter, where she enjoys going on walks and dancing Bomba with a local Puerto Rican cultural dance ensemble.

THANK YOU
AND NEXT STEPS

Thank you for reading my book. This is not the end! The tips and examples shared in my book are your first steps toward getting what you want.

As my gift to you, I encourage you to visit my website, elizabethsuarez.com, to learn more about negotiating throughout your life. You will be able to download the following resources:

An Infographic identifying how to develop your own path.

My How to Undertake a Negotiation video. In this video, I provide techniques on how to have effective discussions during any negotiation or interaction.

Follow me on Twitter @ElizabethSuarez to get some more insights about The Art of Getting Everything.

I welcome the opportunity to speak at your event or organization on the ideas discussed in this book. Please reach out to me via my website at elizabethsuarez.com or by email at elizabeth@elizabethsuarez.com

Remember, you can make your own difference! To your success!

Morgan James
Speakers Group

We connect Morgan James published authors with live and online events and audiences whom will benefit from their expertise.